MW00651758

Published by Northland, A Church Distributed
I Don't Do Crazy Anymore
Copyright © 2011 by Dr. Joel C. Hunter
ISBN: 978-0-615-45018-6

Published by Northland, A Church Distributed

All proceeds go to Northland, A Church Distributed.

I DON'T DO CRAZY ANYMORE!

Why difficult people and circumstances
no longer set the agenda for my life

Dr. Joel C. Hunter

I Don't Do Crazy Anymore is dedicated to my granddaughter,
Ava Belle Hunter, who went to be with Jesus
on September 4, 2010, at the age of five.
As I said at her memorial service, "She lived a life
that didn't just touch people. It changed people.
There will be many more people who will be living life differently,
including her family, because she was here."

◉◉◉

CHAPTER 1

Overcome Evil With Good

Shall we indeed accept good from God and not accept adversity?

Job 2:10

Pain has a way of bringing into focus our picture of who God is. Nobody understood this better than Job, a righteous man in the Old Testament whom God allowed to be tested by Satan. First, the devil took away everything Job had, including his health. Then, everyone in Job's family, save Job and his wife, was suddenly killed. When word came to Job and his wife, they had two completely different reactions. "His wife said to him, 'Do you still hold fast your integrity? Curse God and die!' But he said to her, 'You speak as one of the foolish women speaks. Shall we indeed accept good from God and not accept adversity?'" (Job 2:9-10). I like the King James Version of verse 10 better because there is a great juxtaposition: "Shall we receive good at the hand of God, and shall we not receive evil? In all this did not Job sin with his lips."

So many of us can relate to Job's story. Many of us are going through difficult times right now or have just been through difficult times. Recently, my family went through the greatest trial we have ever faced. On Labor Day weekend 2010, my little five-year-old granddaughter, Ava Hunter, died ... ten weeks to the day after doctors discovered she had a rare form of brain cancer. We had prayed fervently for her healing and were joined by many others around the world. God answered our prayers with perfect eternal healing. He always answers our prayers. He always heals. That is His nature. Still, the pain of missing Ava remains, and it is very real.

During our struggle, we faced crazy circumstances ... and a few crazy people. We learned quickly that in order to survive, we have to have an understanding of who God really is. Many people don't. Job's wife didn't. She was a fair-weather believer: *As long as the weather is fair, I believe. As long as God is blessing me, protecting my family and me, I believe ... because what is God there for except to rescue me and keep me from harm? If God doesn't keep me from harm, then I don't believe in Him anymore.*

Job's wife believed in a very limited God. But Job believed in an ambidextrous God, a God who can work good from evil just as well as He can work from good. He is a powerful God, a good God, a strong God. Therefore, Job was able to say to her, "Wait, are you telling me that we should just accept part of what God has for us, that we should just accept good times and not hard times? That's crazy!" And it's crazy for a five-year-old girl to develop brain cancer, one of the rarest forms in children, and be dead within ten weeks. But it's crazier not to understand that God can work good from evil.

◉◉◉

Whenever we're going through difficulties in life, we're going to face two types of people. One type is going to be like Job's wife, saying, "I don't see how you can still believe in God after going through this." The other type will be like Job's friends were initially and will have sense enough not to comment. Often the very best thing people can do is not say a word, just be there. But even Job's friends eventually couldn't resist, and our friends won't be able to resist either. In Job 4:2, Job's friend Eliphaz says, "But who can refrain from speaking?" Job's friends spoke, and that is what our friends will do. They'll be compelled to try to help by finding either a fault or a solution.

There was a time when Josh and Lisa, Ava's parents, said, "Hey, we are open to any suggestion because this kind of cancer does not respond to traditional treatments." My third son is a medical doctor and went through all the literature. Dr. Francis Collins, director of the National Institutes of Health, connected with me and offered the family his prayers and sympathies, but there were no open protocols on this type of cancer because it is extremely rare, so the traditional treatments of chemo and radiation had little chance of working. Therefore, for a season, Josh invited anyone to offer solutions via his blog. For the most part, people gave great ideas, and Josh and Lisa explored as many of them as they could. But eventually they came to a point where they had to cut off the advice.

When somebody who is going through crazy circumstances cuts off advice, no one should offer advice anymore. No one should ever say to us as we suffer, "If you had only ... ." There should be a penalty for "unnecessary roughness" for anyone who says that because it just loads on guilt. When we are going through hard times, we are doing the very best we can. We never need anyone to say, "I told you so" if the circumstances get worse. There are some people, though, who have a need to place themselves— instead of the suffering folks and God—at the center of the crisis. That's crazy, and we don't need to deal with that. Sometimes we just need to grieve alone with God. Not only is that okay; that kind of time needs to be prized and protected. But there are other times when someone says exactly what we needed to hear—it is a message from Heaven.

After Ava died, many people posted encouraging words and prayers on Josh's blog and on Facebook. One comment was especially helpful to our whole family: "You know, there's never a time when the pain gets any less because for the pain and the sorrow to get less would somehow diminish or dismiss the value of the person. It would make you forget what you had with that person. It would make you forget part of the contribution the person made to your life. No, the pain doesn't get any less, but you get bigger around it." I love that! Our lives get bigger and deeper and better because of the pain.

Do we accept good from the Lord and not evil? No, because He works good out of both. In all that Job went through, he never blamed God, and I can say in all that Ava went through and my family experienced, we never once blamed God either. This is what Job 1:22 says: "Through all this Job did not sin nor did he blame God." Why? Because Job knew we are not made for this world; this world isn't the ultimate point.

Writer and editor Marshall Shelley had a son named Toby who died just two minutes after he was born. Though questions swarmed around his soul in the days following his son's arrival and departure, Marshall eventually concluded that God "didn't create Toby to live two minutes any more than He created me to live eighty years. ... He created each of us for eternity." The length of time isn't the point. What we are made for, to draw near to God and help others draw near to God, is the point. So let's remember what we are made for, but let's remember the goodness of God all the more.

And we never give up asking God for healing or a miracle. My family prayed for Ava's healing to happen here on Earth right up through the last hours of her life. Of course, we wanted a "yes." But we know this about our Father: Even when He answers "no," it is because His "no" is better than our "yes." The Bible says not a hair can fall from our heads without His knowledge of it (Matthew 10:28-30). Do you really think God forgot about Ava? Do you really think He didn't hear our prayers? Jesus taught this about our Father, extrapolated from worldly fathers in Matthew 7:9-11: "What man is there among you who, when his son asks for a loaf, will give him a stone? Or if he asks for a fish, he will not give him a snake, will he? If you then, being evil, know how to give good gifts to your children, how much more will your Father who is in heaven give what is good to those who ask Him!" The principle here is that God's "no" meant He had something better than a "yes" ... better for Ava, better for us, and better for Kingdom purposes.

Somebody who has been in ministry longer than I have wrote to me, with some of Job's friends' words. He wrote, "We all know this wasn't God's will." What? Do you mean to tell me our God is not powerful enough to heal a child's brain tumor if He wants to? The God who rose from the dead can't heal a tumor? Of course He can! This was God's will. And God's will is good because He is as good as He is strong. We have to believe that and refuse to waver. Already we've seen good come out of this. We've seen people's lives changed because of what we've been through. We've seen people come to saving faith in Jesus Christ, and people are continuing to come to the Lord because of Ava. More than two thousand people attended her memorial service, and four thousand people watched online from twenty-eight countries. Thousands more have since watched her memorial service online from all over the world, and person after person has said, "I've come back to God because of her." My son Pastor Isaac Hunter, who officiated the service, summed up her life. He said, "Ava's life was a call to worship."

We've got to know the character of God. We've got to understand who He is so we can walk by faith and not by sight. We've got to not be afraid anymore, and we've got to understand that we, as Christians, are the only people in the world whose God suffered in order to redeem us through suffering. It's not God's will only if we are able to avoid suffering. It's not just God's will if we can escape pain. Redemption is different from rescue. Redemption is deeper, it's better, and it causes us not to be afraid anymore because no matter what happens, we'll come out better because of it.

◉◉◉

We need to understand that the opposite of love is not hate. It's fear. Satan will always try to get us to be afraid. When Jesus walked in this world, He didn't say, "Hate not"; He said, "Fear not." Our enemy is fear. So many people fear illness, or what could happen to their family or those whom they love. And, yes, when circumstances get crazy, those circumstances are for a while intimidating. But my daughter-in-law Lisa said this during this memorial service, which was a deep worship experience for me: "For a long time, I was afraid of getting cancer ... but Ava has taught me there is nothing to be afraid of. Death is not something to be afraid of." Once her daughter got cancer, Lisa wasn't afraid of cancer anymore because God is bigger than cancer, and cancer does not set our agenda.

Satan will always overplay his hand, and he'll take us to the place where we're so beaten down and our face is so in the dirt until we rise up and say to his face, "No more! You will not have control of my life. I will not fear you or anything you can do to me." In all things, "we are more than conquerors through him who loved us" (Romans 8:37, NIV). We've got to know God, and we've got to know who we are in Jesus Christ. When we have that confidence, we're going to laugh even during the hurting times because tragedy will not have its way with us. Even death itself will not have its victory. The grave will not have its sting (1 Corinthians 15:55).

It says in Ecclesiastes 3, there's "a time to weep and a time to laugh" (v. 4). Sometimes those times come together. Don't ever be afraid to laugh in the face of hurt because laughter is the tone of victory over hurt, over depression, over defeat. There's "a time to mourn and a time to dance" (v. 4). Ava loved to dance. One of my favorite moments during Ava's memorial service was when they played her favorite Jackson 5 song. Was that inappropriate? No. That was absolutely appropriate. I bet Ava is dancing even now. "In all these things we are more than conquerors through him who loved us." We can laugh in the face of fear and dance in the time of death because we are not afraid anymore; we are not defeated.

One of my favorite passages in the entire Bible has to do with King David. King David went through a tragedy. He did not live a sinless life; in fact, he sinned big-time. But he loved God, and nothing could dissuade him from loving God fully. The first child of David and Bathsheba only lived a short time, and as a result, David's face was in the dirt. But there came a time when he had to pick himself up. Second Samuel 12:18-20 reads: "Then it happened on the seventh day that the child died. And the servants of David were afraid to tell him that the child was dead, for they said, 'Behold, while the child was still alive, we spoke to him and he did not listen to our voice. How then can we tell him that the child is dead, since he might do himself harm!' But when David saw that his servants were whispering together, David perceived that the child was dead; so David said to his servants, 'Is the child dead?' And they said, 'He is dead.' So David arose from the ground, washed, anointed himself, and changed his clothes; and he came into the house of the LORD and worshiped." By God's grace, David got on with his life. And by God's grace, so will we.

◉◉◉

I've learned some important things from my family's tragedy, and I've decided how I'm going to live from this time on. There are crazy times in this life, and there are crazy people in this life. But I'm not going to set my life according to crazy anymore. In this life, there are natural fears that people have of getting sick or someone they know getting sick, but I want to tell you, I'm not going to be afraid of getting sick ever again in my life because I've seen what it can do and what it can't do, and I'm going to live according to what it can't do. It can't defeat me; it can't stop me from doing good in spite of it; it can't stop God's grace from redeeming the destruction. And to anybody who comes into my life and tries to provoke me into fear about any kind of illness, I'm going to say, "I'm sorry, I don't do crazy anymore."

If we have lived our lives in regret, and every day we remember something we did wrong, something we wish we could do all over again, that's crazy! Why? Because it is telling God that we know more about whether or not we should have forgiveness than He does. It is telling God that we are wiser than He is. It is telling God that we will make a judgment rebutting His when He died on the cross and put to death our sin, our guilt, our fear, our death. It's refusing God. That's crazy, and we don't do crazy anymore!

I know the media get their ratings from crazy. But when I see crazy on TV, I'm going to switch it off because I don't do crazy anymore. The only way to defeat crazy is to "overcome evil with good" (Romans 12:21). Do we know what that means? That means reasonable, sensible people figuring out real solutions.

I don't know how much longer I have in this life—it could be twenty years, it could be twenty minutes, but it really doesn't matter. I'm going to spend that time building a better world for our grandchildren. So I would invite you to not do crazy anymore with me. Let's not let crazy people and circumstances control our lives. Choose life and life more abundantly (John 10:10).

Pray with me ...
God, thank You for Jesus Christ. He is our Hope. He is our Power. He is our Payment. He is our Sanity. Let us fix our eyes on Jesus, the Author and Perfecter of our faith. Let us walk according to faith, not according to sight. Let us build up and not tear down. Let us love and not hate. Let us walk in faith and not fear. In Jesus' name, amen.

CHAPTER 2

Dances With Wolves

Behold, I send you out as lambs in the midst of wolves.

Luke 10:3

There came a time in the life and the ministry of Jesus when He sent out His disciples with the greatest message in the whole world. And while His Kingdom will be established by Him and Him alone, it is to be extended through us—making Earth more like Heaven: "Thy kingdom come, Thy will be done in earth, as it is in heaven" (Matthew 6:10, KJV). Like He did the disciples of old, God is sending us out with a world-transforming message, and we're going to run into some crazy people. But we don't have to be afraid because He is with us.

Remember that Heaven is a matter of nearness and not just a place we will go to someday. Yes, Jesus said, "I go to prepare a place for you" (John 14:2). However, Jesus was talking to people who had a linear perspective. It's imagery that His Jewish listeners would definitely understand. However, Heaven is not just a place; it's a presence. When Jesus said, "The kingdom ... is at hand" (Matthew 10:7) and, "I will be with you always" (Matthew 28:20, NCV), He was talking about the presence of Heaven on Earth. He's talking about being near us, and if

He's near us, then all who are with Him are near us also.

I've learned so many things with the death of my five-year-old granddaughter. There was a time during her battle with cancer when I couldn't think about the future because I couldn't make myself face a time when she wouldn't be here, but I should have known better. Heaven is presence; it's not just an environment. When she is with Him and He is with me, she is with me. In a way, she's closer to me than she has ever been. When the Bible says we are surrounded by "so great a cloud of witnesses" (Hebrews 12:1), it's not just Moses. It's not just David. It's not just Abraham and Isaac and Jacob. It's Ava! It's people who knew the Lord, and they're with Him now, and they're with us now, as we know the Lord.

So we've got the greatest message and the greatest mission in the entire world. He's sending us to everyone, everywhere ... and He's going where we're going because He promised to be with us always. But Jesus also warns us, "Behold, I send you out as lambs in the midst of wolves." It's important to remember that we are the lambs, not the wolves. I want you to write this down in your brain and, even more, in your heart: Bridle your tongue. We cannot advance the Kingdom by attack. It's crazy to try to do it that way, and we don't do crazy anymore. There will be those who attack, and we will be tempted to counterattack. But we're not the wolves; we're the lambs. Frankly, people won't believe we have good news if we wear grimaces on our faces. They won't believe that we have love to share if we're yelling at them. They won't believe that we have the answer to what they've been looking for if they can't stand being with us. We are the lambs. We're not the wolves. Let's never forget that!

◉◉◉

How, then, are we to conduct ourselves as lambs and not wolves? First of all, we can't get distracted. The more we are carrying around, the more we have to pay attention to instead of the Kingdom. When Jesus sent out His disciples, He told them: "Carry no money belt, no bag, no shoes; and greet no one on the way. Whatever house you enter, first say, 'Peace be to this house.' If a man of peace is there, your peace will rest on him; but if not, it will return to you. Stay in that house, eating and drinking what they give you; for the laborer is worthy of his wages. Do not keep moving from house to house. Whatever city you enter and they receive you, eat what is set before you; and heal those in it who are sick, and say to them, 'The kingdom of God has come near to you'" (Luke 10:4-9). In practical terms, that means we are to be humbly grateful, not grumbly hateful.

Jesus also said to look for a man of peace. Who's that? Well, in this context, it's not another Christian because He was talking to His first followers as He sent them out to non-Christians. Even today, it won't always be Christians who treat us with respect and are open to us and to the message we carry. We should not be ashamed that we have friends who aren't Christians. That's great! We've found some men of peace or daughters of peace. The biblical example of this can be found in Acts 10:1-2: "At Caesarea there was a man named Cornelius, a centurion in what was known as the Italian Regiment. He and all his family were devout and God-fearing; he gave generously to those in need and prayed to God regularly" (NIV). Cornelius wasn't a Christian or a Jew. He was a Roman who did not know the real God, but his house was open to inviting the apostle Peter, so Peter went to him. Cornelius began to share his "network" with Peter.

When we have non-Christians in our networks, it's more interesting because we get to connect with all of their friends who are not Christians ... yet. My wife, Becky, and I did this when we moved to Florida, and the church started to grow. Do you know how it grew? We just went to our sons' athletic events, and we'd talk to whomever was beside us. We weren't trying to convert them to Christianity; we were just trying to get to know them. Why?

Because people will never believe the larger message of love unless they sense we love them just for who they are. Phil Cooper, author of the sales book *The Big Kahuna*, said there's a difference between friendship and salesmanship. Whenever we are in a conversation so we can make a "sale"—I don't care if it's Jesus or soda pop— as soon as we try to manipulate that conversation so we can get them where we want them to go, we have ceased to become their friends and have become marketing reps instead.

We don't convert people anyway; God does the converting, and we aren't all that helpful to the process if our only goal is to find a way to work the Gospel into every conversation we have. The first thing we do is love people for who they are, asking them about their families and friends and what they're interested in, and caring about them, even if it never goes anyplace else. God is the Author of transformation and is well able to open up opportunities for us to share His love with others. He loved us for who we were before we ever came to Christ. We have to be able to do that with other people. So, let's look for men and women of peace and just do life together. Eventually, they will see how we live life. The medium is the message. They're not going to listen to what we have to say; they're going to watch how we live. They're going to hear our opinions and how we speak, and then they are going to judge if they want that kind of life. Witnessing is not about what we say; it's about living a life so distinctly that we couldn't possibly live that life unless God existed.

◉◉◉

On our journey, we're going to meet people who aren't people of peace. As a matter of fact, they don't want what we've got, and they don't want us. What do we say to those who reject us? First, we need to understand that the world is crazy in part because that's what we reinforce. Think about it … . Who sets the agenda for our lives? Be honest. It's usually the people who have complained to us. We feel our life's goal is to eradicate their complaints. So the people who run our lives are the complainers. They're the most negative people who see everything that's wrong, and they whine and get angry, and we run around trying to please them. The reason they live that way is they get attention for it—we, as a society, have kind of rewarded and reinforced their behavior.

I heard a story once about a department store that wanted to celebrate its millionth customer. One day a lady walked in, and BAM! Suddenly, cameras were everywhere, and the manager stepped up to pin a rose on her. He handed her one hundred dollars and announced, "You're our millionth customer! What brought you to our store today?" She replied, "I was on my way to the complaint department." That's what we do as a society and a church. Whoever gripes the most is the person who gets our attention! That's crazy, and we don't do crazy anymore. We already have an agenda, and it's a positive agenda! There are problems that need to be solved, but the problems don't determine who we are. Problems don't change us into scared people who are trying to win the approval of people who will never approve of us. That's a crazy way to live. Does that mean we should avoid crazy people? No. Jesus said, "I send you out as lambs in the midst of wolves." There are some crazy people out there, so I'm going to help you to negotiate the wolves.

Counter to anything you may have heard previously, crazy isn't somewhere we go. Crazy is when we build our own world and only listen to "voices" within that world.

Back in the 1960s, I served as a chaplain in an asylum for a year as part of my doctoral program. My first day, I was walking across campus when a lady in a tattered robe sprung out of the bushes and looked at me and said, "I know who you are, and I know what you've been saying about me. I will kill you!" Well, in those days we didn't have post-traumatic stress disorder ... we just went home and changed our pants and thought things over. I soon realized I had seen firsthand the definition of "crazy." This woman most certainly did not know me, I had never said anything about her, and seriously, she had absolutely no reason to kill me. Crazy people are trapped in the conversations inside their own heads. They're hearing voices inside their own heads but are thinking they are hearing the voices outside their own heads. There are groups that are crazy, that think theirs are the only voices that speak the truth. If we dare speak up with another opinion, we're not just different; we're a threat. Such is the crazy voice of paranoia.

We see this in the Bible in the story of King Saul. Saul was King David's predecessor, and David loved him. Saul could not have had a more loyal subject than David. But because of David's military successes, the crowds loved David more than Saul. Instead of valuing David and seeing him as an asset, Saul got paranoid. First Samuel 18:8 says: "They have ascribed to David ten thousands, but to me they have ascribed thousands. Now what more can he have but the kingdom?" David only sought to lift up Saul, but Saul was crazy—paranoid and fearful. The Bible goes on to say, "Saul looked at David with suspicion from that day on" (v. 9).

Have you ever been in a conversation and the person you are talking to just goes off? You wonder what happened to set him off. Everything you accomplish he takes as a personal threat. He takes it as a diminishment of who he is or what he said because he seems determined to have an enemy. We've all got people like this in our lives. What do we do? Change the subject or change geography just for the moment.

Remember the movie *To Kill a Mockingbird*? There is a scene in that movie where Scout, Jem, and Dill are walking in the street past crazy Miss Dubose's house. She's sitting on her porch, as she frequently does, and Jem tells the others not to say anything to her because she'll shoot them just as quick as she looks at them. So they all continue walking ... with Scout, an irrepressible little girl who can't help herself, lagging. She says, "Hey, Miss Dubose!"

Miss Dubose goes off, "Don't you say hey to me, you ugly girl! You say, 'Good afternoon, Miss Dubose!' You come over here when I'm talking to ya!"

Atticus, Scout's dad, sees what's going on and intervenes, saying: "Good afternoon, Miss Dubose. My, you look like a picture this afternoon. My goodness gracious, look at your flowers. Have you ever seen *anything* more beautiful? Miss Dubose, the gardens at Bellingrath have nothing to compare with your flowers." Well, Miss Dubose is so disarmed that she doesn't know what to say and blurts out, "Oh, I don't think they're as nice as last year." He says, "Oh, I can't agree with ya. I think that your yard is gonna be the showplace of this town. Well, grand seeing ya, Miss Dubose." Then he takes the kids and walks away.

I want you to know something about crazy people. We can change the subject on them. If we just change the subject, they'll often go to the new topic right along with us. But we certainly don't need to enter into what they were talking about because we will not argue them out of their point. They're not reacting to us; they're reacting to voices inside their heads. Change the subject or change geography for a while, and they'll eventually simmer down.

◉☉◉

Then there are people who are crazy not because they are fearful, but because they're just satisfied. That was the rich young ruler in Luke 18 who went up to Jesus, wanting another treasure (rich people accumulate stuff; they are not focused on giving). He went up to Jesus and said, "'Good Teacher, what shall I do to inherit eternal life?' And Jesus said to him, 'Why do you call Me good? No one is good except God alone. You know the commandments, "Do not commit adultery, do not murder, do not steal, do not bear false witness, honor your father and mother."' And he said, 'All these things I have kept from my youth.' When Jesus heard this, He said to him, 'One thing you still lack; sell all that you possess and distribute it to the poor, and you shall have treasure in heaven; and come, follow Me.' But when he had heard these things, he became very sad, for he was extremely rich" (vv. 18-23).

There are people who don't want a faith that requires anything from them, but only a faith that adds to them. If that's you, I'm sorry … you've got the wrong religion. Love has a price; it's called pain. Love has a price; it's called inconvenience. Love has a price; it's called putting others before yourself. That's what we do. Love doesn't lord over others; love lifts, and love serves. We are the givers, not the takers. There will be some people who will not follow Jesus because they have perceived correctly that they need to sacrifice in order to do so. People who are crazy-satisfied won't follow Christ until they see something in our lives that they want more than all of the accumulations they have in their own.

◉◉◎

Finally, there are people who are crazy because they are totally self-righteous and spend their time judging other people. These are the people in our lives who will never listen to us because they know our mistakes, and they didn't make those mistakes, so they think they're better than we are. It's like the parable of the Pharisee and the tax collector that Jesus shared in Luke 18: "Two men went up into the temple to pray, one a Pharisee and the other a tax collector. The Pharisee stood and was praying this to himself: 'God, I thank You that I am not like other people: swindlers, unjust, adulterers, or even like this tax collector. I fast twice a week; I pay tithes of all that I get.' But the tax collector, standing some distance away, was even unwilling to lift up his eyes to heaven, but was beating his breast, saying, 'God, be merciful to me, the sinner!' I tell you, this man went to his house justified rather than the other; for everyone who exalts himself will be humbled, but he who humbles himself will be exalted" (vv. 10-14).

We, the lambs, are the ones who realize that none of us is "good enough." We're the ones who say, "I've made all kinds of mistakes, and if I could do some stuff over again, I would." But periodically, we run into voices that try to accuse and blame and work up all kinds of scenarios and conspiracies about other people.

My friend Shelly is a wonderfully bright person who happens to have cerebral palsy, a condition that affects her motor skills such that she can't walk well or speak well. But just to look at her, you really don't notice anything is different. One day she pulled up to a Starbucks and parked in a handicap spot. Out of nowhere, a big, muscular guy came up, banged on her car, and yelled, "Don't you have anything better to do than to just sit in a handicap spot?" Well, I wish he'd have consulted me before he jumped into that hornet's nest because Shelly is a unique character, and she really doesn't take anything from anybody. So she very carefully formed her words so he could understand what she had to say. It didn't take long for the man to recognize that she has a disability, and he just sort of froze up, then turned and walked into the store. A few weeks later, she was back in Starbucks when the guy walked in. Shelly walked over to him and said, "Excuse me, I want to know which vehicle is yours so I can go pound on it." Embarrassed, the man tried to justify himself to Shelly, saying, "Doesn't it make you mad that people park in handicap spots who don't need to, just to run into the store? Doesn't that bother you of all people?" This is what Shelly said: "I don't ascribe to people faults I haven't noticed. They could have a heart problem, they could have an issue with panic attacks, or they could have cerebral palsy. I don't make up my mind about people before I get to know them."

There are people in our lives who have taken on the role of general manager of the universe. Why do we keep trying to please those people? That's crazy! And we don't do crazy anymore. Or maybe we are some of those people trying to manage the universe.

If so, we need to stop that craziness because we don't do crazy anymore. We are the lambs, not the wolves. We are the humbly grateful, not the grumbly hateful. And those in the world are watching to see if there is any chance that someday they might believe.

Pray with me ...

God, help us to take our eyes off of one another and to fix our gaze upon You. Help us to sense Your presence everywhere, every day and to live what we believe. In Jesus' name, amen.

CHAPTER 3

Think Different

Paul was waiting for them at Athens ... reasoning in the synagogue with the Jews and the God-fearing Gentiles, and in the market place every day with those who happened to be present.

Acts 17:16-17

Did you know we are the only people in the world who worship a personal God who is both singular and plural at once? That is unique to us Christians. God said, "Let Us make man in Our image. ... Male and female He created them" (Genesis 1:26-27). So God is a relationship who made us for relationships. But while His is a relationship in perfect harmony—Father, Son, and Holy Spirit—our relationships often are punctuated by disagreement. All of us have "arguers" in our lives, but we don't have to let them drive us crazy because we don't do crazy anymore. In fact, we need to recognize that God sometimes uses arguments and arguers to develop our character and build our endurance.

Some of us have been athletes, and we've had coaches who have said some disrespectful things about us ... and our mothers. What were those coaches trying to do? Were they trying to get us to break down and not perform well? No, they were trying to make us stalwart enough so we could be a solid part of the team and not break down when it counts. Understand? Arguments do that, too. So it can be a good thing when people challenge us because it can make us think, and it can make us strong.

In Matthew 15:22-28, there was a woman who argued with Jesus to heal her daughter. It says: "And a Canaanite woman from that region came out and began to cry out, saying, 'Have mercy on me, Lord, Son of David; my daughter is cruelly demon-possessed.' … And He answered and said, 'It is not good to take the children's bread and throw it to the dogs.'" Ouch! It looks as though Jesus was knocking her down with His words, but in fact, He was trying to build up her faith. It worked! She replied, "'Yes, Lord; but even the dogs feed on the crumbs, which fall from their masters' table.' Then Jesus said to her, 'O woman, your faith is great; it shall be done for you as you wish.' And her daughter was healed at once."

Remember, we will never persuade others of anything from our perspective. We will only be able to persuade them from their perspective. In order to do that, we've got to know what their perspective is. Let me show you Paul's learning perspective in Acts 17:17. He's in Athens—the place where philosophy, religion, and politics were decided in his day. (While we may have heard otherwise, the reality is that politics and religion have been mixing for centuries.) Acts tells us Paul was "reasoning in the synagogue with the Jews and the God-fearing Gentiles, and in the market place every day with those who happened to be present." The Greek word for "reasoning" means looking at a subject from different perspectives, and can be translated as reasoning, debating, or arguing. Paul could reason with anybody because he knew enough about the people to argue from their perspectives. He used their points of view to help them consider the Gospel of Christ. Paul knew arguing is not just waiting our turn so we can have our say; it is actually learning from others because they have a perspective we don't. This not only demonstrated his wisdom, but it also increased his effectiveness. Why? Because if we have a point that's true for everybody, it will be true from other people's perspective as well as ours.

◉◉◉

I've just outlined some of the ways God uses arguments and arguers in our lives, but there are also ways we can argue that will damage our relationships. I want to give you a few "guardrails" to remember. If we keep these in mind, our arguments will be constructive instead of crazy.

1. The person who is disagreeing with us is not our enemy. Ephesians 6:12 says, "For our struggle is not against flesh and blood, but against the rulers, against the powers, against the world forces of this darkness, against the spiritual forces of wickedness in the heavenly places." Therefore, never attack people personally. That's called an ad hominem argument, and it really is not helpful. The weaker our argument, the more tempted we are toward either personal attack or a volume that betrays an emotional unhinging. Getting personal or loud is almost always a sign of a weak argument. We've got to do a gut check and ask ourselves, *Have I stopped addressing the subject and just gone to war with the person?*

It's a benefit if we can talk about something without creating strife. Proverbs 20:3 says, "Keeping away from strife is an honor for a man, but any fool will quarrel." Do you know why I'm not impressed with people in the media who just yell and blame other people and tear other people down? Because any fool can do that. We don't stand up for something by tearing others down; that doesn't make us heroes or virtuous somehow. No, any fool can quarrel. It takes somebody very smart and wanting to be effective for something higher to argue in a way that causes no strife.

James 3:5 says, "So also the tongue is a small part of the body, and yet it boasts of great things. See how great a forest is set aflame by such a small fire!" The most powerful muscle in our body is our tongue. It forms words that can change people's worlds for better or worse. James adds, "No one can tame the tongue; it is a restless evil and full of deadly poison. With it we bless our Lord and Father, and with it we curse men, who have been made in the likeness of God; from the same mouth come both blessing and cursing. My brethren, these things ought not to be this way" (vv. 8-10). Let's watch out that we don't use our tongue for attack or destruction.

2. Arguing can't just be for our emotional release. Displaced anger is when we are frustrated about something, but we take it out on something else. A lot of times when we pick a fight with somebody, it's because we're trying to get the emotions out. I heard a story about a little kid who'd been brought up in a strict family during the Depression. His mother was one who believed children are to be seen and not heard. He got a job selling newspapers and stood out on the sidewalk, yelling, "Get your paper here!" He loved that! He was grinning the whole time. Somebody went up to him and bought a paper and said it looked like he loved his job and that he must sell a lot of papers. He said he didn't sell a lot, but he liked the job because it gave him a place to yell. We are the same way sometimes when it comes to arguing. We just want to yell. But yelling at people will always end in destruction, and it will destroy our relationships.

3. We don't have to win the argument. Sometimes in order to get what we want ultimately, it's important that we don't win the argument. In Mark 9:33-35, the disciples were going to Capernaum, and along the way, Jesus had heard some of them talking. When He asked what they were discussing, the Bible says, "They kept silent, for on the way they had discussed with one another which of them was the greatest. Sitting down, He called the twelve and said to them, 'If anyone wants to be first, he shall be last of all and servant of all.'" Do you know the most effective arguments I've ever participated in are those I chose not to win? I chose instead to learn. I chose to serve and build up someone else, rather than intimidate or overpower the other person.

The reason God allows argument, and sometimes even pushes it, is not just so we can be built up in our personal character and endurance or clarify the issues. It's so we can love others better. Here is the unspoken concern of most arguers: *Can we argue and still have a relationship? Can we argue without your stomping out? Can we argue and know our relationship is more important than any disagreement we could have because I love you whether we agree or not?* That's the point.

Many times people, especially our children, want to know that from us. Many times our friends do, too. I don't know that I've ever been in a congregation where there was as wide a variety of opinions and politics and backgrounds and religious experiences as at Northland. Do you know why we are still together? Because we have one value above all: We know and love Jesus Christ. That doesn't mean we will ever agree on much of anything, let alone everything. What it means is we have a relationship with Him that will keep our relationships with one another secure. It's not about keeping from losing; it's about improving our loving.

Pray with me ...
God, there are many disagreements in the world, both spoken and unspoken. Help us to always value relationship above the argument. In Jesus' name, amen.

CHAPTER 4

Public Enemies

God causes all things to work together for good to those who love God, to those who are called according to His purpose.

Romans 8:28

The Bible says we all have enemies. That's a matter of fact. Romans 12:14 says, "Bless those who persecute you; bless and do not curse." It doesn't say, "If someone persecutes you"; it says there are people persecuting us. Jesus puts it even more plainly in the Sermon on the Mount in Matthew 5:43-45: "You have heard that it was said, 'You shall love your neighbor and hate your enemy.' But I say to you, love your enemies and pray for those who persecute you, so that you may be sons of your Father who is in heaven." He doesn't say, "If you have enemies." He says we have enemies, and we must learn how to deal with them. Our enemies may be unknown to us. They may be terrorists on the other side of the world who hate us because we belong to the "wrong religion" or we live in the "wrong country," or the only reason they hate us is because they don't know us. (I mean, what's not to love about us?) There also may be people who know us and really are trying to take us down. The simple fact is we all have enemies, and we have to figure out how to deal with them so they don't dominate our lives.

The reason we have enemies is God has arranged them for our benefit. Romans 8:28 says, "All things ... work together for good to those who love God, to those who are called according to His purpose." The Spanish philosopher Baltasar Gracián said, "A wise man gets more use from his enemies than a fool from his friends." So what benefit can enemies possibly add to our lives? Consider this: When we are attacked, when we are threatened, when we are hated, the first place we go to is our source of security. Our ultimate security lies in what God has already done for us, rather than in defending ourselves from what other people might do to us. When we are attacked, we rely on God, and we remember, "If God is for us, who is against us?" (Romans 8:31). "We are more than conquerors" (Romans 8:37, KJV). "No weapon that is formed against you will prosper" (Isaiah 54:17).

◉◉◉

Our natural tendency when we've been hurt or threatened by our enemies is to take vengeance. We want to get even. We want to come out on top somehow. That never works. This is what Romans 12:17-19 says: "Never pay back evil for evil. ... Never take your own revenge, beloved, but leave room for the wrath of God, for it is written, 'Vengeance is mine, I will repay.'" Do we really think we can get better vengeance than God can? Do we really think we can make better arrangements for justice than God can? Stop trying. Turn it over to Him. He will repay. That means we need to let it go, and until we do, it will have a hold on us and we will live crazy lives because we are always going over in our minds what we should have said, what we wish would have happened, how we might get even. It holds us in bondage. We are never free until we forgive.

Forgiveness is tough because it's inherently unfair. Why should we, the ones who have been hurt, have to make the effort to be the ones who forgive? But if we don't, then we're the ones who are continuing to be hurt by those who hurt us in the first place. Do we really think our preoccupation with those people is hurting them? It doesn't affect them one little bit. They probably don't care what we are thinking. The only people we're hurting are ourselves. We have to get out of that bondage.

Forgiveness is acknowledging who has hurt us and declaring that we now forgive them. Does that mean we somehow dismiss what they have done to us? No! Does that mean what they did to us was not important? Not at all! Does that mean somehow we have to be reconciled to them and are now their friends? No! It means we have determined, "I am not going to give them power over me anymore. I am not going to let them have my attention. I am not going to be preoccupied with them anymore." When we make that declaration, it is done spiritually. Will a flash memory of it come back? Probably. We may have to renew our forgiveness. Matthew 18:21-22 says: "Then Peter came and said to Him, 'Lord, how often shall my brother sin against me and I forgive him? Up to seven times?' Jesus said to him, 'I do not say to you, up to seven times, but up to seventy times seven.'"

It's like buying a house. When we buy a house, we sign on the dotted line, and legally that's our house. But most of us have to keep making regular payments, so it becomes our house a little more every day, until one day, we have no more payments, and it's fully ours. It's the same with forgiveness. Many times we have to make "payments." That memory will come back, and we will need to say, "No, I have forgiven that person, and I am not going to be preoccupied with that anymore because my life is too important to be re-assaulted by that memory. That person is forgiven." Eventually, it won't come back because we will own the whole forgiveness of the person and event. Does forgiveness cost? It does. But unforgiveness costs way more. And when we don't forgive, it harms our forgiveness with the Lord. In Matthew 6:12, when Jesus taught us to pray, He said, "Forgive us our debts, as we also have forgiven our debtors." In case we miss that correlation, He said in Matthew 6:15, "But if you do not forgive others, then your Father will not forgive your transgressions." Are you really going to let your enemies take away your forgiveness? That's a crazy way to live, and we don't do crazy anymore.

It's our choice. Jesus said in Luke 4:18 that He came "to proclaim release to the captives." Let's not let other people have power over us anymore. Let's not add to the acrimony and the anger and the accusation that already is in the world. Let's not become the bearers of the methods of the enemy. One time I heard a story about a blind man who would go out at night and would always carry a lantern with him. Somebody eventually asked him why he carried a lantern since he was blind. He gave these profound words: "I carry a lantern so that others won't stumble over me." "You are the light of the world" (Matthew 5:14). We have to be careful no matter what our hurts are that people don't stumble over us. We, of all people, should be the ones who build and don't destroy. We, of all people, should be the ones who give hope. Let's make sure we don't choose the dark world of those who tear down; no one should stumble over us.

I know the fantasy we have about people who have hurt us and in our imaginings, we say something so smart that they would be utterly undone. That doesn't happen in reality.

We undo those who would suppress us or diminish us, the same way we defeat evil in this world, by filling the world with so much good that evil is marginalized and helpless. I heard a story that in 2007, there was a "Tube strike" in London (the subway there is called "the Tube"), so there were long lines of people waiting for the busses. A man named Gareth Edwards was standing with other commuters in a long, snaking line, waiting for a bus, when a smartly dressed businessman blatantly cut in line behind him.

(In England, they call it "queue-jumping.") People complained, but the interloper simply ignored them. So this is what Gareth did: He turned to the elderly woman standing behind the businessman and asked her if she'd like to go ahead of him. She accepted, so he asked the person behind her, and the next person, and the next—until sixty or seventy people had moved ahead. Gareth and the seething queue-jumper just kept moving farther and farther backward. When the bus finally pulled up, Gareth heard a shout from the front of the line. It was the elderly woman calling out to Gareth: "Young man, do you want to go in front of me?" That's how we get rid of evil—a little bit at a time. Keep on doing the next right thing, and evil will be powerless because we will have edged it out incrementally.

Pray with me ...
God, we love You. And You promise to work all things together for good to those who love You and are called according to Your purpose. Help us to trust You fully and not do crazy anymore, knowing Your plans will prevail. In Jesus' name, amen.